Portage Public Library

I Can Read, Too

Book 2

Library of Congress Cataloging-in-Publication Data

Sargent, Dave, 1941-
    I can read, too. Book 2 / by Dave and Pat Sargent ; illustrated by Laura Robinson. — Prairie Grove, AR : Ozark Publishing, c2001.
  [24] p. : col. ill. ; 18 x 21 cm. (Learn to read series ; bk. 2)

    SUMMARY: Tells what a variety of animals can do, such as a snail crawling, a whale blowing water, a wolf howling, and a horse bucking.
  ISBN: 1-56763-579-2 (hc)
        1-56763-580-6 (pbk)

  [1. Animals—Fiction.] I. Sargent, Pat, 1936- II. Robinson, Laura, 1973- ill. III. Title. IV. Series.

PZ7. S2465Icb 2001
[E]—dc21   00-012635

Copyright © 2001 by Dave and Pat Sargent
All rights reserved

Printed in the United States of America

I Can Read, Too

Book 2

by Dave and Pat Sargent

Illustrated by Laura Robinson

Ozark Publishing, Inc.
P.O. Box 228
Prairie Grove, AR 72753

Dave and Pat Sargent, authors of the extremely popular Animal Pride Series, plus many other books, visit schools all over the United States, free of charge.

If you would like to have Dave and Pat visit your school, please ask your librarian to call 1-800-321-5671.

On the last page is a list of vocabulary words and the number of times each word is used.

Portage Public Library

wolf

catfish

snail

shark

whale

seal

sand dollar

beaver

horse

I am a wolf.

I can howl.

I am a catfish.

I can swim.

I am a snail.

I can crawl.

I am a shark.

I have sharp teeth.

I am a whale.

I can blow.

I am a seal.

I like to play.

I am a sand dollar.

I like the sand.

I am a beaver.

I can cut with my teeth.

I am a horse.

I can buck.

Below is a list of 29 vocabulary words and the number of times each word is used.

word	count	word	count	word	count
a	9	like	2	wolf	1
am	9	my	1		
beaver	1	play	1		
blow	1	sand	2		
buck	1	seal	1		
can	6	shark	1		
catfish	1	sharp	1		
crawl	1	snail	1		
cut	1	swim	1		
dollar	1	teeth	2		
have	1	the	1		
horse	1	to	1		
howl	1	whale	1		
I	18	with	1		

Portage Public Library

31814 88050130 6

Sargent, Dave
I can read, too. Book 2

DATE DUE

8/2004

E
S

Sargent, Dave
I can read, too
Book 2

Portage Public Library